DESIGNER

Nail Charms

Lisa Mallett-Zimmerman

hinkler

Published by Hinkler Books Pty Ltd
45–55 Fairchild Street
Heatherton Victoria 3202 Australia
www.hinkler.com

Author: Lisa Mallett-Zimmerman
Internal design: Trudi Webb
Cover design: Mandy Norman
Editor: Kayla Clibborn
Art Director: Paul Scott
Photography: Hinkler Studio
Illustration: QBS Learning

ISBN: 978 1 4889 1821 6
Printed and bound in China

Contents

About This Book

This book is all about creating beautiful nail art on your very own fingertips! It contains useful information about your nails and how to care for them. It also takes you through the skills and techniques required to create works of art on your nails with the use of nail polish, charms, gems and stickers. It then guides you through 12 nail art designs: from sweet treats to summer fruits, mermaids to cute kitties. These dazzling designs will add style and personality to your look!

To create the projects in this book you will need:

- ✿ Nail clippers
- ✿ Nail file
- ✿ Nail buffer
- ✿ Large bowl
- ✿ Warm water
- ✿ Soap
- ✿ Towel
- ✿ Cuticle stick
- ✿ Hand cream
- ✿ Nail polish remover
- ✿ Nail polish
- ✿ Scrap paper
- ✿ Scissors
- ✿ 2 x 8 cm (3.1 in) gold chain

In Your Kit:

- ✿ Set of 10 clear press-on nails with adhesive
- ✿ Set of 10 painted press-on nails with adhesive
- ✿ 1 x bottle of clear nail glaze
- ✿ 1 x roll of holographic striping tape
- ✿ 1 x dual-ended dotting tool
- ✿ 1 x sheet of 50 assorted nail stickers
- ✿ 150 x assorted flat clay charms
- ✿ 250 x nail gems including diamantés and pearls in assorted colours and shapes

All About Nails and Nail Care

Nail care involves a healthy diet and regular manicures.

A Healthy Diet for Healthy Nails

The following foods are great for your nail health:

- Fruit – especially strawberries, blueberries and bananas
- Leafy greens – especially spinach, kale and broccoli
- Vegetables – especially sweet potatoes, carrots and tomatoes
- Nuts and seeds – especially almonds and sunflower seeds
- Beans and legumes – especially lentils
- Whole grains like brown rice and oats
- Lean meats and salmon
- Milk
- Eggs

Nail Files

Nail files are tools that grind and shape the edges of nails. They can be ceramic, glass or metal, or made of emery board, with surfaces ranging from coarse to fine. Coarser surfaces are used to shorten and shape nails quickly, and finer surfaces are used to smooth and shape nail edges.

Cuticle Sticks

Hoof sticks and orange sticks are used to gently push back your cuticles (the skin at the base of the nail) from the base of the nail.

Nail Buffers

Buffing helps your nails to grow as it increases the flow of blood in the nail beds. Buffing also takes off the dull top layers of the nail and builds up shine. This leaves a smooth surface ready for polish.

Nail Scissors

Nail scissors have short, slightly curved blades. They are very sharp, so be careful when using them. Nail scissors are used mainly to cut the length of a nail, before the shaping is done with a file.

Cuticle Cream/Oil

These treatments are used to soften the cuticle. They come in a variety of forms, so you can choose the one that works best for you.

Manicures

A manicure is a great way to prepare your nails for nail art creations. First you trim, shape and polish your nails, then moisturise your skin.

You Will Need

- ✿ Nail clippers
- ✿ Nail file
- ✿ Nail buffer
- ✿ Large bowl
- ✿ Warm water
- ✿ Towel
- ✿ Cuticle stick
- ✿ Hand cream

1. Trim all of your nails to the desired length with the nail clippers.

2. Shape all of your nails with the nail file. File your nails in one direction and create either square or rounded tips.

3. Polish your nails with the nail buffer. Glide the buffer gently across the surface of your nail to smooth and polish it.

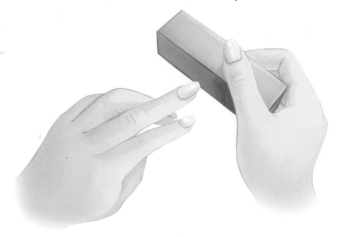

4. Soak both hands in a bowl of warm water for at least two minutes, then dry your hands with the towel.

6. Polish your nails again with the nail buffer.

5. Gently push back the cuticles from your nail with the cuticle stick.

7. Moisturise your hands by gently massaging hand cream around the skin of every nail and the rest of your hands.

Nail Art – Getting Started

Nail Art involves painting, decorating and embellishing the nails. Nail art is not a new idea: humans have been decorating their nails for a long time! Paintings found in ancient Egyptian tombs from 2330 BCE show people with painted nails.

Nail Polish

Nail polish comes in just about any variety you could wish for! All the colours of the rainbow are readily available, plus a variety of finishes, such as gloss, matte, glitter and metallic. You can purchase nail polish from a wide range of shops, like chemists, department stores and beauty stores. Or you could ask very nicely to borrow some from your friends or family!

Nail Charms

Nail charms come in a wide variety of metal, plastic and clay charms. They also come in a range of fun themes, like sweet treats and summer fruits.

Nail Gems

Nail gems come in a wide range of colours and shapes, sometimes referred to as diamantés. Gems are usually glued to the nail but some are self-adhesive.

Nail Stickers

Nail stickers are just stickers that have been specifically designed to fit on the nail. You could practically use any sticker, as long as it fits on your nail.

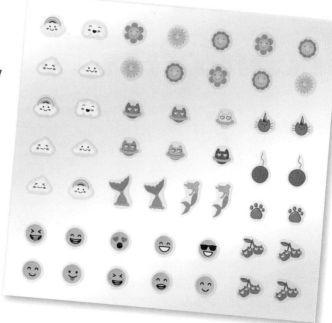

Press-on Nails and Nail Wheels

Press-on nails are fake nails that are either clear, painted or completely painted and decorated. They come on a nail wheel, which allows easy nail polish application, and decoration with charms, gems and stickers. They are self-adhesive and can be stuck on and taken off as you please!

Nail Art Techniques

How to Apply Nail Polish

The following steps apply to both base coats of colour and top coats of clear nail glaze.

1. Wash your hands with soap, ensuring your nails are cleaned, then dry with a towel. If you wish, perform a manicure on yourself (refer to page 7 on manicures).

2. Apply a thin layer of your chosen nail polish. Make the first brush stroke through the centre of the nail, starting at the bottom edge of the nail.

3. Make a second and third brush stroke up the left and right sides of the nail.

4. If you get nail polish on your skin, take a cotton bud, dip it in nail polish remover and wipe clean the nail polish on the skin.

5. Allow ten minutes for the nail polish to dry. This is often the hardest step! There is not much you can do without knocking your nails and smudging your nail polish, so try to sit tight!

6. If a second coat is required, repeat steps 2 to 5.

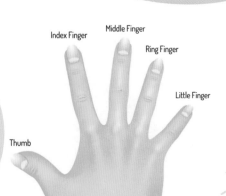

Handy Hint

Ensure there is not too much nail polish on the brush by wiping the brush against the inner edge of the bottle.

Fingernail Notation

Throughout this book the names of each fingernail will be referred to as follows:

Index Finger
Middle Finger
Ring Finger
Little Finger
Thumb

How to Remove Nail Polish

1. Soak cotton wool in nail polish remover.

2. Press the cotton wool onto your nail for a few seconds, then wipe off the nail polish.

3. If you are not using an acetone-free remover, apply baby oil to your cuticles to protect them from drying out.

Salvaging Smudges

Dip your finger in some nail polish remover and rub it over the smudged area of the nail. Take your nail polish colour and go back over the area. Apply a top coat to smooth everything over. Simple!

Handy Hint

If you're working with peel-off nail polish, you don't need to use nail polish remover. Simply pick at the edges of your base nail polish until you can carefully peel off the whole nail polish layer!

How to Create Patterns

Dots

To create perfect dots, the dotting tool is an essential! Take your chosen nail polish and drop a small amount onto a scrap piece of paper. Dip the dotting tool into the nail polish, then dot the nail with the dotting tool. It's that easy!

Handy Hint

Many household items can be used as dotting tools, for example, pen or pencil tips, bobby pins, sewing pins and toothpicks. You can create dots of varying diameters if you find dotting tools with different widths – see what you can find!

Stripes

To create the straightest of stripes, striping tape is your answer!

The striping tape in this kit can be used in two different ways:

1. The tape is holographic, so you can apply it to your polished nails in different patterns to achieve holographic stripes. After laying the tape in position, you trim the ends overhanging the skin around the nails for a neat finish.

2. Use the tape as a masking tape by applying it to areas you don't want painted. You then paint over the top of the tape and only the areas not taped will be painted. Remove the tape to leave the stripe pattern behind.

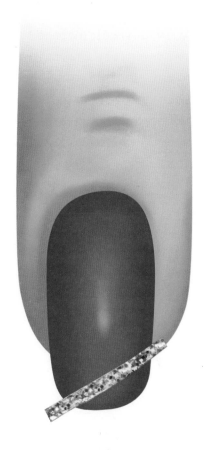

How to Fix Nail Charms and Gems

Apply clear nail glaze to the bottom side of a charm or gem, then place it on your nail. If you have them, small tweezers can be used for picking up and placing nail charms and gems. The dotting tool can also be used to nudge the nail charm or gem into the correct position – if you use your fingers, they will inevitably end up all sticky with glaze! Once the glaze has dried and all decoration is complete, add a final top coat of glaze to the entire fingernail.

How to Apply Nail Stickers

Nail stickers are super easy to apply: simply peel off the sticker sheet, line it up in the correct position on the nail and press down. If you have them, small tweezers can be used for picking up and placing the nail sticker.

How to Fix Press-on Nails

Press-on nails are fixed to your nails once they have been painted, decorated and given a top coat. You simply detach each press-on nail from the wheel and place the double-sided adhesive sticker on the bottom side of it. Then press each nail down onto your own nails, ensuring you match up the correct size with each fingernail. You can choose any of the projects in this book to decorate the press-on nails instead of your own nails.

Confetti Bling

The simplest of patterns can be so effective! These dazzling confetti dots are a great beginners design to build your nail art skills.

You Will Need

- ✿ Soap
- ✿ Towel
- ✿ Nail polish (white, light blue, light pink and light purple)
- ✿ Round gems (blue, pink, green and purple)
- ✿ Clear nail glaze
- ✿ Dotting tool
- ✿ Scrap paper

1. Wash your hands with soap, ensuring your nails are cleaned, then dry with a towel. If you wish, perform a manicure on yourself (refer to page 7 on manicures).

2. Apply two base coats of white nail polish to your thumb and ring finger nails, light blue nail polish to your index finger nails, light pink nail polish to your middle finger nails and light purple nail polish to your little finger nails (refer to page 12 on how to apply nail polish).

Handy Hint

Ask a friend or family member to help you to polish the nails of your dominant hand or your writing hand. It can be very tricky to paint your own nails with the non-dominant hand!

3. Take the round gems and stick them to your thumb and ring finger nails (refer to page 16 on how to fix nail gems). Randomly spread the gems out and use approximately the same number of each gem colour on each nail. The number of gems you use will largely depend on the size of your nails.

5. Apply a top coat of clear nail glaze (refer to page 12 on how to apply nail polish).

Ba-da-bling!
Your confetti bling nails
are a celebration of colour
and sparkle, right on your
fingertips!

4. Using the dotting tool, paint different coloured dots on your thumb and ring finger nails (refer to page 14 on how to create patterns). Randomly spread the dots out and paint approximately the same number of each dot colour on each nail.

Butterflies in the Garden

This nature-inspired design will brighten your day with butterflies fluttering around your fingertips amidst a leafy garden. If you love all things natural and pretty, then this look is for you!

You Will Need

- ✿ Soap
- ✿ Towel
- ✿ Nail polish (light blue, white and light green)
- ✿ Clay leaf charms
- ✿ Clay butterfly charms
- ✿ Clear nail glaze
- ✿ Dotting tool

1. Wash your hands with soap, ensuring your nails are cleaned, then dry with a towel. If you wish, perform a manicure on yourself (refer to page 7 on manicures).

2. Apply two base coats of light blue nail polish to your thumb and ring finger nails, white nail polish to your index and little finger nails and light green nail polish to your middle finger nails (refer to page 12 on how to apply nail polish).

Try This!

You can add to this design by painting on little leaves with a nail polish colour of your own choice.

1. Take your dotting tool and make a dot on your nail (refer to page 14 on how to create patterns).
2. Take a sewing needle and, starting at the centre of the dot of paint, drag the needle outwards in a slight curve. This will make a leaf shape! Add several little leaves over just one nail in particular, or all of them!

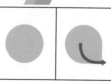

3. Take the clay leaf charms and stick a few of them to the bottom of each of your thumb nails. Then take the clay butterfly charms and stick a couple of them to the top of your thumb nails, as though they are flying above the leaves. The number of charms used will largely depend on the size of your nails (refer to page 16 on how to fix nail charms).

4. Take the clay butterfly charms and stick a few of them to each of your ring finger nails .

5. Take the clay leaf charms and stick a few of them to each of your middle finger nails.

6. Stick one clay butterfly charm in the centre of the index and little finger nails.

7. Apply a top coat of clear nail glaze (refer to page 12 on how to apply nail polish).

Well done! Now you can enjoy watching the butterflies fluttering through the leaves on your very own fingertips!

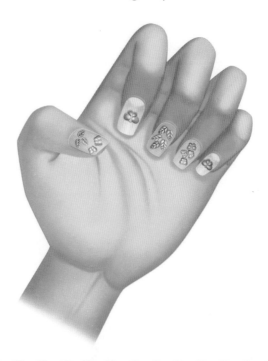

Tutti-Fruity!

This design is a bright burst of fruitilicious fun!
You'll love pairing this look with a colourful summer outfit.

You Will Need

✿ Soap

✿ Towel

✿ Nail polish
(light orange, light green,
light pink and lime green)

✿ Clay fruit charms

✿ Clear nail glaze

✿ Dotting tool

1. Wash your hands with soap, ensuring your nails are cleaned, then dry with a towel. If you wish, perform a manicure on yourself (refer to page 7 on manicures).

2. Apply two base coats of light orange nail polish to your thumb nails, light green nail polish to your index and little finger nails, light pink nail polish to your middle finger nails and lime green nail polish to your ring finger nails (refer to page 12 on how to apply nail polish).

3. Take the clay fruit charms and stick a few of them to each of your thumb nails. Fit on as many as you can here to make it look like a real fruit salad! (Refer to page 16 on how to fix nail charms.)

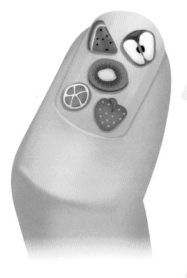

4. Stick one clay fruit charm in the centre of your index, middle, ring and little finger nails.

5. Apply a top coat of clear nail glaze (refer to page 12 on how to apply nail polish).

Voila! Your tutti-fruity creation is a fruit salad of fabulous!

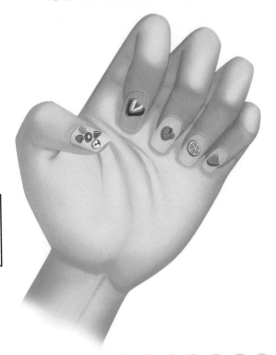

Try This!

Try painting some little cherries throughout this design with your dotting tool and a sewing needle.

Sweet Treats

This yummy design is full of your favourite sweet treats! For all the sweet tooths out there, this is the delicious decoration your nails need.

You Will Need

❀ Soap

❀ Towel

❀ Nail polish (light pink, light blue, light yellow and white)

❀ A mix of sweet clay charms like cupcakes, lollies, icy poles and hearts

❀ Clear nail glaze

❀ Dotting tool

❀ Scrap paper

1. Wash your hands with soap, ensuring your nails are cleaned, then dry with a towel. If you wish, perform a manicure on yourself (refer to page 7 on manicures).

2. Apply two base coats of light pink nail polish to your thumb and ring finger nails, light blue nail polish to your index and little finger nails and light yellow nail polish to your middle finger nails (refer to page 12 on how to apply nail polish).

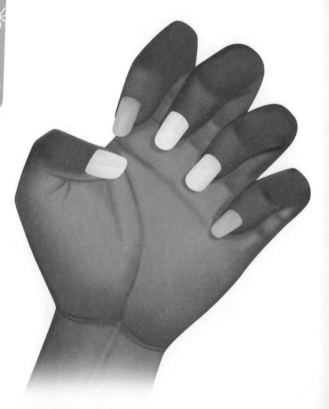

3. Take the clay cupcake charms and stick a few on each of your thumb nails. The number of charms used will largely depend on the size of your nails (refer to page 16 on how to fix nail charms).

4. Take two clay icy-pole charms and stick one on each of your index finger nails.

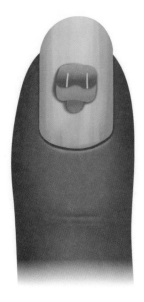

5. Take two clay ice cream charms and stick one on each of your ring finger nails.

6. Take four clay heart charms and stick one on each of your middle and little finger nails.

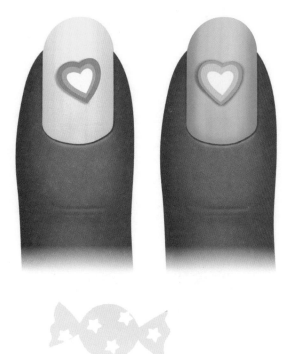

7. Using the dotting tool, paint white dots on your index and ring finger nails (refer to page 14 on how to create patterns). Randomly spread the dots out on each nail. Allow the dots to dry.

8. Apply a top coat of clear nail glaze (refer to page 12 on how to apply nail polish).

Try This!

There are a range of cool nail charms available in craft shops like these chunky sweet treat nail charms.
Try re-creating this design with chunky plastic nail charms that really pop!

Wow!
Your colourful sweet treats are a delicious addition to your look!

Dazzling Doughnuts

This quirky doughnut design is visually appealing and appetising!
The chunky nail charms, pastel colours and candy stripes
are a dazzling doughnut delight.

You Will Need

- ✿ Soap
- ✿ Towel
- ✿ Nail polish (light blue, light yellow, white, light pink and neon pink)
- ✿ Striping tape
- ✿ Scissors
- ✿ Chunky or flat clay doughnnut charms
- ✿ Clear nail glaze
- ✿ Dotting tool
- ✿ Scrap paper

1. Wash your hands with soap, ensuring your nails are cleaned, then dry with a towel. If you wish, perform a manicure on yourself (refer to page 7 on manicures).

2. Apply two base coats of light blue nail polish to your thumb and little finger nails, light yellow nail polish to your index finger nails, white nail polish to your middle finger nails and light pink nail polish to your ring finger nails (refer to page 12 on how to apply nail polish).

Handy Hint
Make sure that the nail polish is completely dry before you remove the striping tape. Remove the tape very slowly and with care to ensure nice neat stripes.

3. Apply striping tape to the thumb and middle finger nails. Apply in a vertical pattern for the thumb nails and a horizontal pattern for the middle finger nails (refer to page 15 on how to create patterns).

6. Using the dotting tool, create candy stripe patterns on the index, ring and little fingers. Do this by using the dotting tool like a pen. Use light blue and neon pink for the index fingers, light blue and light yellow for the ring fingers and light yellow and neon pink for the little fingers.

4. Apply white nail polish to the thumb nails and light blue nail polish to the middle finger nails. Once the polish is dry, remove the striping tape.

7. Apply a top coat of clear nail glaze (refer to page 12 on how to apply nail polish).

Fantastic work!
Your dazzling doughnut nail art is as sweet as you are.

5. Take four doughnut charms and stick them in the centre of the thumb and middle finger nails (refer to page 16 on how to fix nail charms).

Happy Clouds and Rainbows

This colourful design will really brighten up your nails! With its cute clouds and beaming rainbows, it has a real wow factor.

You Will Need

- ✿ Soap
- ✿ Towel
- ✿ Set of 10 clear press-on nails with adhesive
- ✿ Nail polish (neon pink, light orange, light yellow, light green, light blue and light purple)
- ✿ Happy cloud stickers
- ✿ Clay rainbow charms
- ✿ Clear nail glaze
- ✿ Dotting tool
- ✿ Scrap paper

1. Wash your hands with soap, ensuring your nails are cleaned, then dry with a towel. If you wish, perform a manicure on yourself (refer to page 7 on manicures).

2. Take the clear press-on nail set and apply two base coats of neon pink nail polish to the thumb and little finger nails, light blue nail polish to the index finger nails, light yellow nail polish to the middle finger nails and light orange nail polish to the ring finger nails (refer to page 12 on how to apply nail polish).

3. Using the dotting tool, create the rainbow pattern on the thumb nails. Do this by using the dotting tool like a pen. First dip the dotting tool in nail polish, then dot onto the nail and follow through with a rainbow curve. The base coat is already neon pink so begin with light orange. Let the nail polish dry before following on with light yellow, light green, light blue and then finally light purple.

Handy Hint

It will help to practise the rainbow pattern on paper first. Then have a go on the press-on thumb nails. If you make a mistake, you can always start fresh by removing the nail polish with nail polish remover.

4. Fix the happy cloud stickers onto the thumb, index, ring and little finger nails. On the thumb nails, place the sticker just below the painted rainbow (refer to page 16 on how to apply nail stickers).

5. Take two clay rainbow charms and stick one on each of the middle fingernails (refer to page 16 on how to fix nail charms).

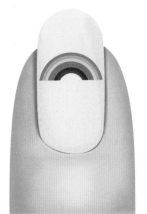

6. Apply a top coat of clear nail glaze to the press-on nails (refer to page 12 on how to apply nail polish).

7. Fix the press-on nails (refer to page 17 on how to fix press-on nails).

How lovely! Your happy clouds and rainbows are ready to brighten up your day!

Mermaid Glamour

This gorgeous mermaid design is for those who love the ocean and its mythical creatures. Its glittering metallic stickers and charms make it a real show-stopper!

You Will Need

❀ Soap

❀ Towel

❀ Set of 10 jade green press-on nails with adhesive

❀ Nail polish (silver glitter and gold glitter)

❀ Mermaid stickers x 2

❀ Mermaid tail stickers x 2

❀ Silver nail gems x 2

❀ Dotting tool

❀ Clear nail glaze

1. Take the jade green press-on nail set. Fix the two mermaid stickers to the thumb nails (refer to page 16 on how to apply nail stickers).

2. Fix the two mermaid tail stickers to the middle finger nails. Take the two silver nail gems and fix them to the mermaid tails between the tail fin and the body (refer to page 16 on how to fix nail gems).

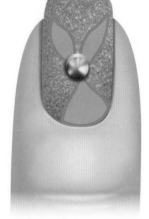

3. Use the dotting tool and gold glitter nail polish to paint the mermaid scale pattern on the index finger nail. Do this by painting a crosshatch pattern of gold lines like the picture below, with the green nail showing through.

4. Repeat step 3 on the other index finger nail and the two little finger nails.

5. Repeat step 3 on the two ring finger nails but with silver glitter nail polish. Then, apply a top coat of clear nail glaze to the press-on nails (refer to page 12 on how to apply nail polish).

6. Before fixing the press-on nails to your own nails, wash your hands with soap, ensuring your nails are cleaned, then dry with a towel.

7. Fix the press-on nails (refer to page 17 on how to fix press-on nails).

Gorgeous work!
Your mermaid nail art is a magical underwater world of glitter and sparkles!

Try This!

You could try this mermaid design on your own fingernails and with a different colour scheme. A glittery turquoise blue, light purple or pink would look great! You can also find chunkier mermaid charms in many craft stores, to use in place of the gold mermaid stickers.

Cosmic Sparkles

This sparkling space-inspired nail art creation is filled with gorgeous nail charms and gems, representing all of the stars and planets in a glittering night sky.

You Will Need

- ❀ Soap
- ❀ Towel
- ❀ Nail polish (purple metallic, silver glitter and light blue)
- ❀ Striping tape
- ❀ Scissors
- ❀ Pearl nail gems x 2
- ❀ Blue square nail gems x 6
- ❀ Silver star nail charm x 8
- ❀ Clear nail glaze
- ❀ Dotting tool

1. Wash your hands with soap, ensuring your nails are cleaned, then dry with a towel. If you wish, perform a manicure on yourself (refer to page 7 on manicures).

2. Apply two base coats of purple metallic nail polish to your thumb and ring finger nails, light blue nail polish to your index and little finger nails and silver glitter nail polish to your middle finger nails (refer to page 12 on how to apply nail polish).

Handy Hint
When applying striping tape, lay the end at the bottom of the nail and run it up to the tip of the nail. This allows you to trim the tape at the tip of the nail, which is much easier and safer than taking the scissors to the bottom edge of the nail where it meets with your skin. Alternatively, you could cut the striping tape to the exact size before positioning it on the nail and sticking it down.

3. Apply striping tape to the thumb nails in an eight-pointed star shape, with the centre in the bottom left corner of the nail (refer to page 15 on how to create patterns).

4. Take two pearl nail gems and fix one to each of the thumb nails at the centre of the eight-pointed star. Then take six silver star nail charms and scatter three on each thumb nail (refer to page 16 on how to fix nail gems and charms).

5. Apply striping tape to the index, middle and little finger nails as one central vertical stripe. Then take six blue square nail gems and fix one of them to the centre of this vertical stripe on each nail.

6. Take two silver star nail charms and fix one to each of the ring finger nails in the top right-hand corner. Then apply striping tape in the shape of a shooting star tail.

7. Apply a top coat of clear nail glaze (refer to page 12 on how to apply nail polish).

Totally awesome!
These cosmic sparkles
are out of this world!

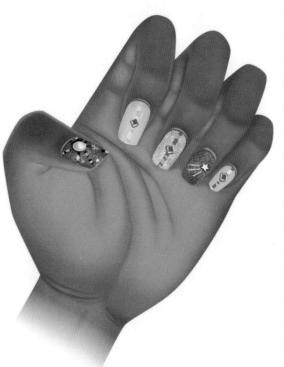

Pretty Charms

This stylish nail art piece represents all of the little treasures you may find in a jewellery box, put out on display on your lovely nails!

You Will Need

- ✿ Soap
- ✿ Towel
- ✿ Nail polish (light orange pearl, gold glitter and white pearl)
- ✿ Pearl gems x 2
- ✿ 8 cm (3.1 in) gold chain x 2 (recycle an old unused necklace of your own or ask an adult if you can use something from their jewellery box)
- ✿ Gold-and-pearl flower charm x 2 (you can create your own flower from individual pearls, gems or beads)
- ✿ Clear nail glaze
- ✿ Dotting tool

1. Wash your hands with soap, ensuring your nails are cleaned, then dry with a towel. If you wish, perform a manicure on yourself (refer to page 7 on manicures).

2. Apply two base coats of light orange pearl nail polish to your thumb and ring finger nails, gold glitter nail polish to your index and little finger nails and white pearl nail polish to your middle finger nails (refer to page 12 on how to apply nail polish).

Handy Hint

If you have them, use tweezers to pick up and position the gold chain. The dotting tool is also very useful for nudging the chain into the correct position. Avoid using your fingers if you can – they are way too big for this finely detailed work!

3. Take two pearl gems and fix one to each of your thumb nails at the centre (refer to page 16 on how to fix nail gems).

5. Take the two gold-and-pearl flower charms and fix one to each of your ring finger nails.

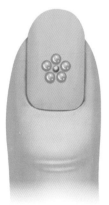

6. Apply a top coat of clear nail glaze (refer to page 12 on how to apply nail polish).

4. Take one of the 8 cm gold chains, place it on a scrap piece of paper and paint it with clear nail glaze. Position the chain on your thumb nail: starting at the tip of the nail, gently drop the chain in place around the pearl charm, wrapping it twice, then take it back up to the tip of your nail again. Repeat this step for your other thumb nail.

Fantastic work!
Your pretty charms are ready
to style with your favourite
outfit and accessories!

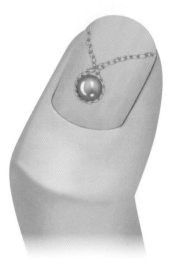

Curious Kitties

This colourful collection of curious kitties is one for all the cat lovers out there. The playful images of these furry, purry friends are quirky and fun!

You Will Need

- ✿ Soap
- ✿ Towel
- ✿ Nail polish (light pink, red and gold glitter)
- ✿ Planet kitty stickers x 6
- ✿ Kitty paw stickers x 2
- ✿ Kittycorn stickers x 2
- ✿ Kitty cherry stickers x 4
- ✿ Ball of wool stickers x 2
- ✿ Dotting tool
- ✿ Scrap paper
- ✿ Striping tape
- ✿ Scissors
- ✿ Clear nail glaze

1. Wash your hands with soap, ensuring your nails are cleaned, then dry with a towel. If you wish, perform a manicure on yourself (refer to page 7 on manicures).

2. Apply two base coats of light pink nail polish to all of your finger nails (refer to page 12 on how to apply nail polish).

Try This!

If you want to try something a bit more challenging, try to paint on your own cute kitty designs. If you search the internet you will find many funny and quirky kitties like purrmaids, batcats, cool cats and dinocats. If you have a fine paintbrush and a little bit of patience, the options are endless!

MEOW

3. Using the dotting tool, paint gold dots on your thumb and red dots on your index and ring finger nails (refer to page 14 on how to create patterns). Randomly spread the dots out on each nail.

4. Apply striping tape to the middle and little finger nails (refer to page 15 on how to create patterns). Apply the tape in opposite diagonal patterns, then apply gold nail polish to these nails. Once the polish is dry, remove the striping tape.

5. Take six planet kitty stickers and stick three of them to each of your thumb nails (refer to page 16 on how to apply nail stickers).

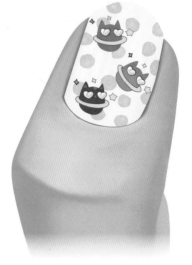

7. Take two kittycorn stickers and stick one them to each of your middle finger nails.

6. Take two kitty paw stickers and stick one of them to each of your index finger nails.

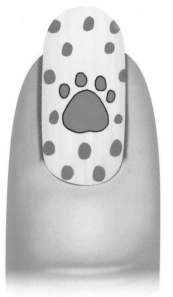

8. Take four kitty cherry stickers and stick two of them to each of your ring finger nails.

9. Take two ball of wool stickers and stick one of them to each of your little finger nails.

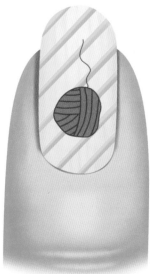

Wow meow!
Your curious kitty creation is totally paw-fect!

10. Apply a top coat of clear nail glaze (refer to page 12 on how to apply nail polish).

Cute Creatures

Adorn your nails with this cute collection of creatures!
This bright and fun design is perfect for animal lovers.

You Will Need

❀ Soap

❀ Towel

❀ Nail polish (white, neon pink, neon orange and neon yellow)

❀ Cute animal clay charms

❀ Clear nail glaze

❀ Dotting tool

❀ Scrap paper

1. Wash your hands with soap, ensuring your nails are cleaned, then dry with a towel. If you wish, perform a manicure on yourself (refer to page 7 on manicures).

2. Apply two base coats of white nail polish to all of your fingernails (refer to page 12 on how to apply nail polish).

3. Using the dotting tool, create a gradient of dots in neon pink, orange and yellow. Make your gradient denser at the bottom and less dense towards the nail tip (refer to page 14 on how to create patterns).

Handy Hint

If you don't have neon nail polish, use gel pens! They are available in lots of shops and come in a great range of colours. They can be used as a substitute for the dotting tool and nail polish here.

4. Take two cute animal clay charms and fix one of them to each of your thumb nails at the centre (refer to page 16 on how to fix nail charms).

5. Take two cute animal clay charms and fix one of them to each of your index finger nails.

6. Take two cute animal clay charms and fix one of them to each of your middle finger nails.

7. Take two cute animal clay charms and fix one of them to each of your ring finger nails.

8. Take two cute animal clay charms and fix one of them to each of your little finger nails.

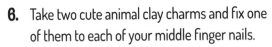

9. Apply a top coat of clear nail glaze (refer to page 12 on how to apply nail polish).

Great work! Your creatures are like a handful of fluffy cuteness ready to be adored!

Emoji Fun

Express yourself with emoji fun! Match your nail art emojis with your own personal happy, silly or funny emotions.

You Will Need

* ✿ Soap
* ✿ Towel
* ✿ Nail polish (gold glitter, white pearl and white)
* ✿ Emoji clay charms or stickers
* ✿ Clear nail glaze
* ✿ Dotting tool
* ✿ Scrap paper
* ✿ Striping tape
* ✿ Scissors

1. Wash your hands with soap, ensuring your nails are cleaned, then dry with a towel. If you wish, perform a manicure on yourself (refer to page 7 on manicures).

2. Apply two base coats of gold glitter nail polish to your thumb and ring finger nails, white pearl nail polish to your index and little finger nails and white nail polish to your middle finger nails (refer to page 12 on how to apply nail polish).

3. Take the emoji clay charms or stickers and fix a few to each of your thumb nails in an even, random spread (refer to page 16 on how to fix nail charms).

4. Fix an emoji sticker to each of your middle fingers (refer to page 16 on how to apply nail stickers).

5. Apply a top coat of clear nail glaze (refer to page 12 on how to apply nail polish).

Try This!

You can play with this design by adding a dot or stripe pattern to each nail first, then adding a range of big and small emojis on top.

Yay! Your emoji fun nails are an animated way to express all your cheerful and silly emotions!

Nailed it!
Where to from here?

Now that you have completed all of the projects in this book and have perfected your nail art skills, you should try your own ideas. Get your imagination going and create your own designs! Start by thinking about your own personal style, and themes that match your personality.

The possibilities are endless! It could be a theme that's really quirky, too. Maybe you don't find the cute and fluffy creatures of the world so appealing, and your favourite thing in the whole wide world right now is insects, or reptiles! So why not cover your fingernails in bugs and scaly critters?

Once you have decided on a theme, think about what nail charms, gems or stickers you can use that match this theme. You may have materials around the home already that may be useful. You should definitely ask for an adult's permission before rummaging through your house for long lost treasures. It is also very environmentally friendly to recycle and upcycle things that may otherwise have been thrown into landfill. You may, however, like to browse your local craft shops, two-dollar shops or department stores for supplies.

Once you have decided on a theme and have gathered some supplies to get you started, the next step is to sketch a design for each nail. Remember all of the skills you have learned and incorporate these skills in your design. Good luck, and have fun!

Theme Ideas

✿ Favourite food

✿ Favourite pet

✿ Favourite animal

✿ Favourite cartoon character

✿ Favourite toy

✿ Favourite sport

✿ Favourite sporting team

✿ Favourite movie/TV show

✿ Favourite game

✿ Favourite musician or band

Skills You Have Learned

✿ Applying base coats with coloured nail polish

✿ Creating patterns using dotting tools

✿ Creating patterns using striping tape

✿ Applying nail charms, gems and stickers

✿ Applying top coats and nail glaze

✿ Using press-on nails

Get Creative!

Once you have a design that you love, start creating your very own personalised nail art on your fingertips! Have fun with your friends too by making up designs together and helping each other paint your nails. It's a great way to spend time with all of your pals. Use the template on the next page to start creating your own incredible designs!

Template